LIMBO TALES

Len Jenkin

BROADWAY PLAY PUBLISHING INC
New York
www.broadwayplaypublishing.com
info@broadwayplaypublishing.com

LIMBO TALES

© Copyright 2014 by Len Jenkin

All rights reserved. This work is fully protected under the copyright laws of the United States of America. No part of this publication may be photocopied, reproduced, stored in a retrieval system, or transmitted, in any form or by any means, electronic, mechanical, recording, or otherwise, without the prior permission of the publisher. Additional copies of this play are available from the publisher.

Written permission is required for live performance of any sort. This includes readings, cuttings, scenes, and excerpts. For amateur and stock performances, please contact Broadway Play Publishing Inc. For all other rights please contact the author c/o B P P I.

First printing: February 2014
I S B N: 978-0-88145-554-0

Book design: Marie Donovan
Page make-up: Adobe Indesign
Typeface: Palatino
Printed and bound in the U S A

ABOUT THE AUTHOR

Len Jenkin's plays include DARK RIDE, TIME IN KAFKA, AMERICAN NOTES, PILGRIMS OF THE NIGHT, CARELESS LOVE, MY UNCLE SAM, LIMBO TALES, PSALM 151, and LIKE I SAY. His works for the stage, often directed by him, have been produced throughout the United States, as well as in England, France, Denmark, Germany and Japan. His adaptations for the stage include Voltaire's CANDIDE (Guthrie Theater, Minneapolis), Aristophanes' THE BIRDS (Yale Repertory Theater, New Haven), and Kafka's A COUNTRY DOCTOR (Classic Stage Company, New York).

His novel *N Judah* is currently available in bookstores and on the web at lenjenkin.com. He has also worked in television and for feature films.

He has received three OBIE awards for Directing and Playwriting, a Guggenheim Fellowship, a Rockefeller Foundation Award, a nomination for an Emmy Award, the Helen Merrill Award, and four National Endowment for the Arts Fellowships.

He teaches in the Dramatic Writing Department, Tisch School of the Arts, New York University.

LIMBO TALES was first presented by Pequod Productions, at the Westbeth Theatre Center, opening on 4 December 1980. The cast and creative contributors were:

MASTER OF CEREMONIES....................................John Nesci
DRIVER.. William Sadler
MAN..Will Patton

Recorded voices ....Richard Bright, Len Jenkin,
Carol Kane, Gerald Marks,
Nancy Mette, Charles Saaf,
Dale Soules & Richard Zobel

Director, costumes, sound, & lights ....Len Jenkin
Set design ....John Arnone

CHARACTERS & SETTING

MASTER OF CEREMONIES
DRIVER
MAN IN HOTEL ROOM

There are also a number of characters who appear as voices, over speakers, radio, through walls, etc. These can be pre-recorded, or live.

A highway
A hotel room

See descriptions in text for more specifics. Individual productions are not meant to follow these stagings, but to use them as indication of mood and style, and then go their own way. There is no "place" given for the MASTER OF CEREMONIES, *other than on stage. There might be a particular set for him, and he might reappear in some guise or perform some function during "Highway" or "Hotel" —those notions should be resolved in their own way by individual productions.*

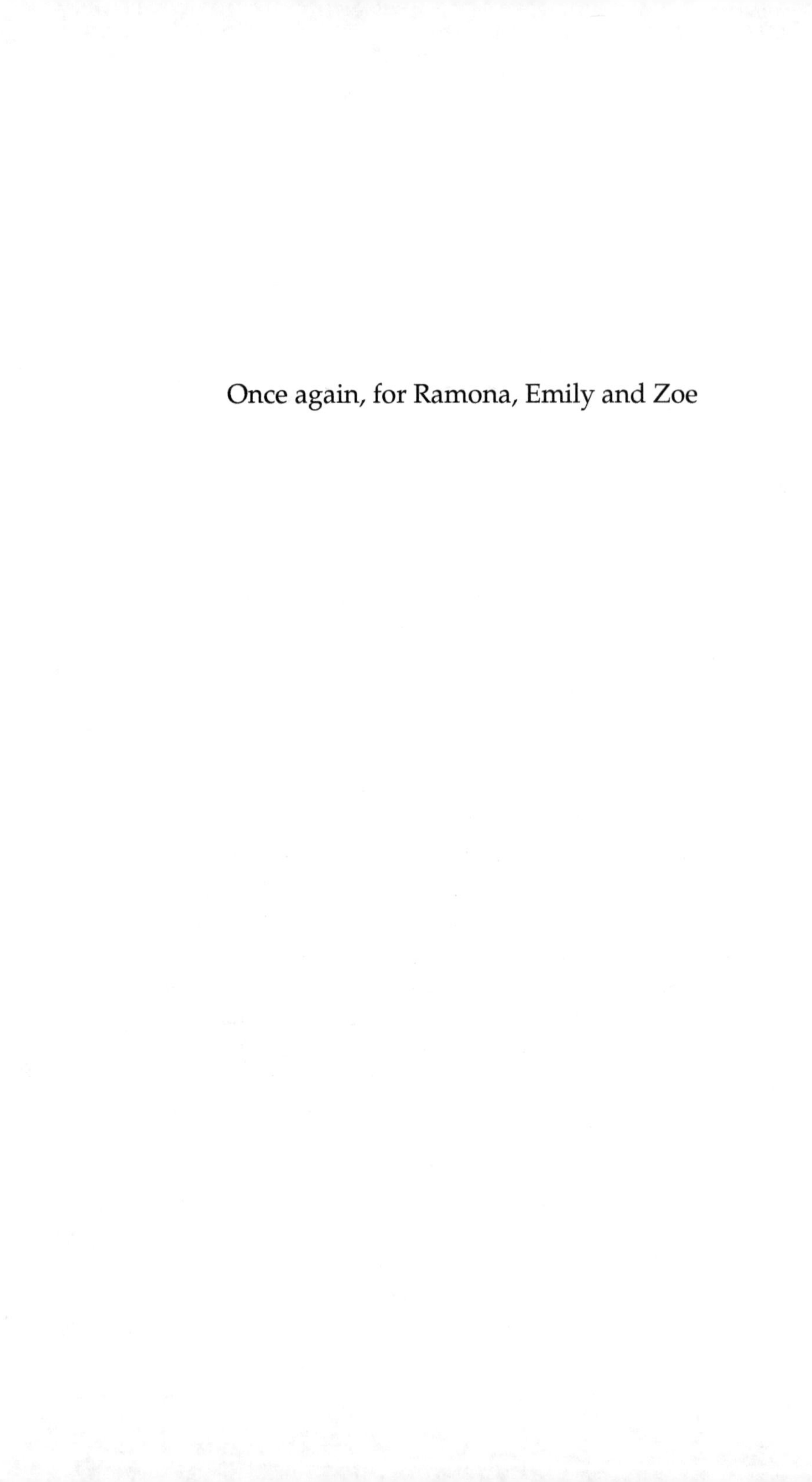

Once again, for Ramona, Emily and Zoe

(The MASTER OF CEREMONIES *enters. He wears a cheap suit and tie. He talks directly to the audience, sinister and slow.)*

M C: Ladies and gentlemen, good evening. And welcome to Limbo Tales. My associates, and I, wish you an enjoyable evening. Good luck. And now, Limbo Tales, Part One. *(He slowly puts on a pair of driving gloves. He mimes driving. A look of sudden terror crosses his face.)* Highway.

HIGHWAY

(The M C *is gone. The lights go to black, come up to reveal the highway set onstage, a very long table, covered by a drop. The* DRIVER *appears, removes the drop. On the table is a miniature highway. It is a two lane road, dotted white line at its center, perfectly straight, perhaps in perspective. The* DRIVER *will move about it as he talks. Structures, vehicles etc. appear during the play as the* DRIVER *describes them, Events occur on set as the* DRIVER *describes them Some occur which he does not describe. Most of these visuals are created directly by the* DRIVER, *by moving models by hand, or by mechanical or electric switches. Some seem to occur by themselves. Lighting indicates evening.)*

DRIVER: Highway. *(He places a small house on one end of the set.)* This is Margaret's house. *(He places a small house on the other end of the set.)* This is my house.

(Lights dim to night, as tiny lights inside the houses come on. The DRIVER *stands at one end of the highway, behind his house.)*

DRIVER: I'm an assistant professor of anthropology at the State University here in Townsend, I hesitated tonight before taking my car out of the garage to make the two hour drive to Bellingham. I've got an end-of-term lecture to deliver in the morning, and the call I received from Margaret was ambiguous, to say the least. She seemed angry about something. I think she said she wanted to discuss our future, or the future, and we had to get together right away. It was a bad connection and her voice was fuzzy, fading in and out. I remember asking if it could wait, and then either she hung up on me, or we were disconnected. I checked my watch—ten fifteen exactly. I tried to call her back in Bellingham and her line was busy. Either she'd taken the phone off the hook, which she's been known to do, or she was calling some bartender she met in the shopping mall. Actually, I doubt that. Our relationship has been pretty strong…Well, I have to admit its been strained a bit lately. My work's been piling up, and the two hour drive between us seems longer… In any case, my lecture isn't till noon tomorrow, so I grabbed my computer with the audio file of my notes, and jumped into the car.

(The DRIVER *places his car on the highway. As we go on, he moves it, and other objects and vehicles, as the text indicates. Or perhaps they move themselves—or a combination of the two…)*

DRIVER: I started this drive at 10:19 P M. There by midnight if I push it—we can talk, and I can be home by four. Or maybe I'll stay over in Bellingham, drive back in the morning. I hope this isn't going to be the kind of serious argument Margaret's been prone to lately. Hell, maybe the whole business is trivial—nothing. I'll get there and she'll wonder why I rushed over…

Driving at night is strange, particularly over a rout you're very familiar with. You see the landmarks you know come up out of the dark: Coppertone billboard, glow of a T V inside a certain house, diner, phone booth, factory, red exit lights on the landings, the quartet of gas stations on the four corners of one intersection: Exxon, Shell, Gulf, Mobil—luminous signs turn slowly in the air. At night the world is blanked out, except for these lit landmarks, and those few signals on which your life depends: white stripe on the blacktop, headlights, taillights, roadsigns. Ignore them for more than two or three seconds and you die. Pay attention to the lights in the dark...and yet, as all those other external signals disappear there's more and more room for internal signs to float up in the dark space the night makes in your mind... Better prep that last lecture. Just get some of these ideas in my head, and I'll be able to wing it...

(The DRIVER *hits "play" on his computer.)*

DRIVER: *(Voice on computer)* Yeah...uh... Final lecture notes, 12:48 A M, Anthropology 201, The Ancient Mayans. From Father Diego Vasquez, "Indians of the Central Americas," chapter three...ah, ah! O K. Once the Mayans constructed their great pyramid at Uxmal, on top of it was stationed a man, chosen by lot, called the Illum Kinnal, the Time Watcher. His job is to protect the sequence of orderly time, to keep it running smoothly from past to future. He does this by guarding it with his eyes. If his attention weakens for one moment, there is a subtle break in the time line. Past, present and future mix, Work in the fields stops. People have visions, headaches, hallucinations. The priests notice the slip-up, and the Illum Kinnal is killed, his heart offered to the gods, and he's replaced by another time watcher...

DRIVER: I don't think I'll mention it to Anthropology 201, but the truth is that the Mayans were nuts. Ten-thirty. Damn phone connection. Did I tell Margaret I was coming? I can't remember...and if I did I can't be sure she heard me. Knowing Margaret, if she doesn't know I'm on my way, she's likely to hop in her car and come rushing over to my house... *(He places Margaret's car on the road near her house.)* That's a possibility. Can't make out the cars, much less who's at the wheel. If one of these sets of headlights coming at me is her, we'll arrive at each other's empty houses... Jesus. That busy signal when I tried calling her back—she could've been trying to call me to tell me she's on her way. If she's coming this way, she'll just put the pedal to the floor. If she arrives at my place and I'm not there, she'll be furious... The last thing I need is a scene the night before my lecture...maybe I should turn around now, go home myself in case...
Hell, I'm working myself up over nothing. She must know I'm coming. She's probably pacing the living room at her place right now, waiting for me.

(The DRIVER *turns on car radio.)*

RADIO: *(Helicopter sounds)* ...This is Celeste from the W Q E Z copter, and it's a beautiful night up here, Bob, visibility unlimited. I can even see the planet Venus along the horizon, and not a traffic flow problem in sight. Bridges and tunnels are good, and the highway between Townsend and Bellingham is clear sailing. So to all you folks at home, and to those folks still on the road, this is your eye in the sky reminding you to drive safely. *(Music follows, rock and roll)*

DRIVER: Uh oh. Low on gas...I'm in luck. Station ahead.

(The DRIVER*'s car moves to model gas station.)*

DRIVER: *(To station attendant)* Ten dollars worth of regular please.

ATTENDANT'S VOICE: *(Offstage or recorded)* You got it.

(The DRIVER *takes out a cellphone, tries to call...)*

DRIVER: My cellphone's dead. *(To* ATTENDANT*)* Say, is there a pay phone around?

ATTENDANT'S VOICE: Yeah. Its out of order.

DRIVER: Look, I have a very important call I have to...

ATTENDANT'S VOICE: Use the one in my office. Near the coffee shop.

DRIVER: Thanks.
(He dials on gas station phone, listens, hangs up.)
No answer. She must be in her car and on the way. All right. All I have to do is turn around and go home, meet her there. I can still get there a good half-hour ahead of her. Might as well have a coffee here. I could use one.
(He puts coffee cup on highway table, sips, opens computer, hits play.)
Ah...let's see what else we've got for tomorrow.

DRIVER: *(Voice on computer)* ...Kornfeld's "Time and the Gods," page 6 of the intro... The Maya conceived of the divisions of time...days, hours, seconds, months, years, as weights carried on the backs of divine bearers. In our terms its as if on, lets say April 26, 1981, there are five bearers in action: the god of number 26 with April on his back, the god of number one carrying the millennium, the god of number nine loaded with centuries, and the god of number eight the decades, and the god of zero carrying the years. At the end of the day, as the date is changed, the gods change. *(Turns off computer)*
Odd notion when you think about it, the gods all members of this gigantic relay team, marching on through eternity. Better hit the road, or Margaret'll get to my place before me...

(He might move cars to illustrate the following:)

Uh oh, what if she stopped on the highway, like I did, and called my place. No answer. She'd figure I was on my way to see her, and she'd turn around to get back to her place before I got there. If that's true—right now we're racing away from each other in opposite directions, to end up exactly where we started. She's impulsive, but she's not dumb. She'd think to call, I better make a U…

God. What if she's realized I'd stop on the road to call too, get no answer, figure she's coming, and go home myself. Then she'll make her U-turn, we pass each other in the night, she ends up at my house, I'm at hers. Nobody home. We turn, race back, pass each other again, and again, and again, and…

This kind of thinking is pointless. All we have here is two people trying to find each other…on a highway at night, true. I am going to stop making circles in my head and just go to her… *(Sings)* Hit the road, Jack, and don't you come back no mo', no mo', no mo'….

You know, from within my Dodge Dart, the world is just pictures, a movie through the windshield. I can change the landscape's soundtrack with a simple flick of the wrist…

(He changes radio stations.)

WBAZ…

WQET…

WKIT…

WETC…

RADIO: "…London at midnight, a great city wrapped in a shroud of dense yellow fog. The streetlights, weird as elfin lamps, grow misty as something fashioned in a dream. Behind an ancient wall, a vast gloomy mansion crouches like an evil beast of prey. On the drawn shades, the shadow of a superman of incredible genius, possessing a brain like Shakespeare and a face like Satan…

(Demonic laughter, and underneath, a drum, continuing….)

DRIVER: I like that. Simple. Boom, boom, boom,…. Hey? What the hell's that rattling around…sounds like something in the glove compartment.
(He takes out a bone flute.)
What the hell is this thing? Who the hell's been driving this car besides me? Nobody, and I cleaned out this glove compartment last week. Some of my students must be playing some kind of practical joke…

*(*DRIVER *plays a few notes on the flute…lovely and mysterious. Drums continuing, and fading)*

DRIVER: Not bad.
Well, back to work. *(Hits play)*

DRIVER: *(Voice on computer)* The Mayans wanted badly to know which gods were marching on any day, because given this information they could define the combined influence of all the marchers of the day, for good or evil, on whatever they wanted to do. The priests did this figuring, but their calculations were far more intricate than you might imagine. Not only the gods of numbers, carrying years, minutes and centuries were marching. They had a cycle of nine nights, over each of which a god ruled. Each lunar phase and each revolution of Venus had its divinity. Then there were gods of the particular activity planned. If they were planting—the soil gods, rain gods, corn gods.

DRIVER: If they were driving, the tire gods, the god of the highway, the gasoline god, and the transmission gods, one for each gear…

DRIVER: *(Voice on computer)* All these gods had to be taken into account, and their attributes, and their relationships to each other, before a prophecy about the probability of success of an action could be arrived at. Handling all these complex and shifting variables was a difficult business.

DRIVER: I bet... *(Hits off)*
I just realized something about those crazy bastards. Like the mapmaker who wanted to make the most accurate map of the world, and kept making it bigger and bigger, and when his map got a mile square, he realized the best map of the world was the world itself—so the job was done. A little tough to read, but that wasn't his trouble. Mayans work the same way. They figured every thing and every concept had its spirit, and they figured it in dee-tail. The world is nothing but a picture made by the combined activity of all the gods in action at this moment. No above, no below. Just here, and the gods are everywhere.
I don't even know if I'm coming or going, or Margaret's coming or going, but it doesn't seem to matter too much at the moment. I'm driving. If I'm in luck I'll find here there. If not, I'll just drive back and forth between Bellingham and Townsend forever.
(Something appears on the highway...or does it?)
Hey...there's a guy on a bike. Or a kid. What's he doing on the highway near midnight?
Hey!
HEY KID!

(Screach of breaks, and then silence. DRIVER *takes a flashlight, searches the table/highway.)*

DRIVER: God. Where the hell is he? I was sure I hit him. Can't even find the damn bike. Nothing anywhere... Uh oh...see-ing things. Or not seeing things.
Hell, this one's better in my head than splattered all over the road. Better take it easy... *(Drive resumes.)*
Crazy priests and their calculations, doping out the future. If the gods looked good, fine. If the situation

looks lousy, the rules are simple. Gods need human blood to give them strength to do their work in the world…and they pay off devout donors in good fortune.

(The base of a Mayan pyramid appears on the highway.)

DRIVER: Better take it easy. "Bellingham, sixty miles." Halfway. You know, this sounds crazy, but when I get there, I don't want to find Margaret home. If she's there—the argument, bitter and no doubt inconclusive. Then lukewarm sex, and sleep. No. What I want is for Margaret to have joined me on the road, racing toward me, and away, and to me again, her Chevy Chevette doing eighty, radio full blast. Both of us racing through the night, secretly hoping never to catch up to each other, desires and doubts become flashes of passing light and steel.

(Another layer of the Mayan pyramid appears.)

DRIVER: Hey, that's funny. The mileage gauge is stuck…or its going too slow to see. I'm still doing sixty, the landscape is still passing the window, but it seems static, featureless…as if I'm on a circular track…and time is…time is…

(The Mayan pyramid is complete.)

STRANGE VOICE FROM EVERYWHERE: Going to paradise is good, and to fall into hell is also a matter for congratulations.

(A thin trickle of blood runs down the side of the pyramid.)

DRIVER: Thou gods, lords of the mountains and valleys, I have given thee to drink. Tomorrow is again day, again light of the sun. I do not know where I shall then be. I am only a traveler. I pass beneath thy hands, beneath thy feet.

Hey…where am I? My head feels like a bomb blew inside. Hey! Is that Margaret's car? There, across the highway? I can pull over…

(He waves frantically.)

Margaret! Here! I'm here! Here!

(Darkness)

INTERMEZZO

(The highway and the DRIVER *are gone.)*

(The M C *enters, same cheap suit and tie. He holds up a hand for silence.)*

M C: Ladies and gentlemen. At this time, I'd like to mention to you those fabulous attractions who were unable to be with us this evening. My associates, and I, combed the fashionable boulevards and back alleys of this great nation, attempting not only to locate these stellar performers, but to lure them to this very stage. However, booking the great and near-great is difficult, not only because of their inflated and insane demands, but due to the fact that most of them have given up on the show business. Lack of appreciation and comprehension on the part of the public has caused them to lapse into a life of aimless musing and despair. We were also hampered, as you might imagine, by our lack of funds, and the condition of this shabby venue. Hard luck dogged our footsteps. Our failure was complete.

We contacted Baron Capiletto, the Italian midget who is not only no taller than the average cigar, but can, and will, open his mouth, and for the pleasure of the viewers, jump down his own throat. He was insulted when we proposed he appear on this program. The little bastard was insulted. Couldn't move him.

We planned to negotiate with Doctor Wu, the Oriental dental artiste. The doctor's act is to painlessly extract the teeth of any member of the audience, shake them up in a bag, load them in a little cannon of his own invention, which he then fires at the head of the volunteer, who miraculously finds all his teeth in place again, whiter and brighter than ever. We finally got the Doctor's unlisted number, only to discover his phone had been disconnected. Couldn't reach him.

We tracked Art Hubble to his trailer camp in Florida. He turned us down flat. He wanted big bucks, the pig. A genius, however.

Hubble is known in the trade as the Human Balloon. He just lies down onstage, and swallows the business end of a tire pump. Then a member of the audience pumps, and pumps, and Art's belly swells, and swells, until you're sure he's gonna explode, and the crowd is screaming "Stop! Stop!" and Art is saying "Keep pumping, you bastard!" Well, you're not gonna see that one.

I personally met with the great Count Orloff, in his room in the Hotel Rio, in the heart of New York's theatre district. The count is ossified and transparent. You can watch his blood circulate, and a copy of the Daily News, held across his back, can be read through his chest. Old man now. He was born in Budapest. When he was in his teens he collapsed one day, bones so soft he couldn't stand. They got him into a chair, and he never left it. The Count has always been in pain, smokes opium constantly to relieve his suffering. Showed himself around the world for sixty years. I begged him to make his comeback in this very show. No luck. Permanently retired.

We also failed to obtain the services of the Bold Grimace Boy. It's a shame you won't see him. He has a tongue about a foot long, can turn one eye out and the other in at the same time, make his face about as small as an apple, then push his mouth out about six inches and shape it like a bird's beak, with eyes like an owl's. To end the act he twists his face up in some kinda way, that damned if he doesn't look like a corpse that's been buried fifty years. Nice guy, too.

Then we thought of adding some kind of scientific exhibit to the evening—giant spider display—freak baby show—or a waxworks. We saw one of those that was something special. Guy has it in a barn up in New Hampshire. He bought it from a Chink who made it back in the thirties. A brass plate in front reads "Mukden, 1937". That's in China. It's a street scene after a Japanese bombing. Regular blood show, but the modeling is really fine. Those statues even have nostril hairs. About ten figures, all wounded and in agony, a pregnant woman, a child, an old man, one guy with his guts bursting out of him, all of them lying there like broken rubble. They just lie there in this barn, and the cows wander in and moo into the dusty Chinese faces, all twisted up with pain. The owner wouldn't rent, and he wouldn't sell.

However, we did manage to obtain one fascinating historical exhibit. See this box?

(He holds up a small box.)

Inside this box rests the iron fly of John Molitor, greatest work of art of this or any age. He was a watchmaker from Bremen. That's in Germany. He's dead now. He made this fly for fun. When he let it out, it just buzzed around the room like the real thing, but if it landed on your hand you knew something was funny. Its heavy. This very fly flew to meet the Emperor Maximilian on his arrival in Bremen on June the seventh, 1840. Molitor figured he'd surprise the Emperor with something special. The Emperor just

reached out and swatted it with his left hand. He wore a yellow glove.
The fly's been busted ever since. It looks like a dead fly in a box. Not worth showing to you, really.
(He slips the box into his pocket.)
Thank you. Thank you all very much. Intermission.

INTERMISSION

HOTEL

(The M C *returns. He wears a hat, and is carrying a shabby suitcase. He lights a cigarette, sinister and slow)*

M C: Ladies and gentlemen, welcome back. And now, my associates, and I, present, Limbo Tales, Part Three: Hotel.

(The M C *is gone, and the Hotel set is revealed.)*

(A MAN *is in a cheap hotel room. The room is very small. On the far side of each of the side walls that enclose the room and its occupant, large audio speakers,* SPEAKER A *and* SPEAKER B. *These two speakers provide the sound from the rooms on either side of the one we see. Each* SPEAKER *has a small light on it that goes on when it is active. The* MAN *hears these sounds through the walls.)*

(The man is reading the Gideon Bible. A window shade is drawn down over a window behind him. There is a suitcase. A circular fluorescent overhead lights the room harshly. There is a telephone. A wilted plant is on the windowsill. The man is dressed in a rumpled suit and tie. Street sounds, dim and far away. The man closes his book, looks out at the audience.)

MAN: The toilet's down the hall, and the landlady's got a padlock on it. She won't gimme the key. So I'm forced, you understand. I am not an animal, but I piss in her goddamn hallway just the same. I'd piss in here if I still didn't have a little while to go. I paid a week when I moved in. Time was up today at noon. Check out time. I'm still here, for the moment. I can't pay any more cause I don't got it. What I got is the clothes I'm wearing, my sample suitcase, one plant from Woolworth's, and three dollars fifty cents ready cash, which is gonna go as soon as the delivery guy from Wong Lo's Chinese take-out place gets here with my food. I gotta eat something...

It ain't like she's got a big crowd waiting for this room. "What am I supposed to do," I tell her, "sleep in the street?" "Yeah" she says, "My ex-husband, for one, does it every night, and he's a better man than you." I thought maybe if I came on to her—she's about fifty, wears this filthy pink housedress all the time and fat, but I figured I could do it, and then she'd let me stay till I figured out where to go...

(SPEAKER A*'s light goes on.)*

SPEAKER A: *(Sound of light snoring begins, fades, begins again, continuing...)*

MAN: ...and then I thought how am I gonna figure where to go? What's the difference. Nothing to figure. I don't need any time. Just waiting a little bit, and then I walk out the door. I don't want to get thrown out of here by the cops. I am not an animal. I'm a man, spelled M, A, N. Man. I tell you this cause I don't know if you'd know by looking.

It goes to show you. If you don't have the smooth tongue of a clever man, or the beauty of a successful whore, its hard to get away with it in this generation. Hard work and dumb love won't do you, my friends, and that's a fact. I don't like to say it, but it's so.

You sign in to this hotel, you sign your name on water. "You got a name?" she says to me at the desk. "Damn right I do" I told her. "I not only got one, I know it by heart." "Sign it then," she says, "but it don't get you nothing. Name or no name you pay in advance. I deal with transients only." "Fine with me," I tell her, "I'm just here temporarily." "That's what they all say" she says. So I'm starved, stalled, and stranded, only this is not the depression so there's no excuse. This is modern times...

SPEAKER A: *(Snoring louder for a moment, then subsides...)*

MAN: However, I'm not alone. I got neighbors, and these walls are made of low-grade cardboard. *(He gestures toward* SPEAKER A.*)* One crazy writer who talks to the furniture—sleeping at the moment—and the other one— *(He gestures toward* SPEAKER B.*)* —a girl. I never see either of them. Only hear them through the walls. *(The man listens.)*

(SPEAKER B *lights up.)*

SPEAKER B: *(Sound of steps. Then they stop. Coughing, very harsh. Then the voice of* SHELLY. *She's eighteen.)*

SHELLEY: (B*)* Shit. *(She coughs again, then silence.)*

(Street noise rises, then falls away... Shadow of a pigeon on the shade behind the MAN, *and then its gone.)*

MAN: My mother died when I was ten. My father never married again, brought me up himself. Five years ago he died. Some kind of blood clot on the brain. I never understood, really. He was coming home from work, and he fell down, and he never got up. Fifty-five years old. So, then I got lonely, and I married Eileen. Had a baby boy, and then I got this selling job, and I was away a lot. I heard she met some guy in the shopping mall who was real good-looking, or funny, or something. I don't know, really. I was sending money home all the time, so Eileen must have liked the other guy a lot, cause that money must have made her feel bad...

SPEAKER B: *(Humming of a little song, coughing, very soft...continuing and fading...)*

MAN: …She should have, too, cause all I thought of on the road was her and the kid.

I'd been away two months one time. When I came back, they were gone. I heard about the guy from the neighbors—got an address too, and I kept sending money for the kid. But I never went there, cause I was scared to. Then I asked in one letter if I could visit. I never got an answer, but the checks kept getting cashed. I guess she didn't want to cash 'em but she had to. Then one of my letters came back with the money still in it. Return to sender, address unknown. So now I don't know where they are or even if they're alive. That was two years ago. So, this is it. This is no song and dance about a hotel room. This is a hotel room.

(A knock on the door. The MAN *opens it. An hand extends through the door holding a brown paper bag. The* MAN *takes the bag, puts money in the hand. The hand withdraws. The* MAN *closes the door, opens the bag: two egg rolls, wonton soup, a fortune cookie. He begins to eat.)*

(Note: During all sound from SPEAKERS A *and/or* B, *the* MAN *in the room, though he may be occupied with what else he's doing, is also listening intently.)*

SPEAKER A: *(Sound of snoring rises, and then stops. Noises of someone getting up out of bed. The voice we hear from this speaker is that of an older man, strong and melodious: the writer.)*

WRITER (A): My god! It's all there! Floating perfect inside my head! I see it all. Am I awake? I've dreamed poems before, but this is extraordinary. I remember every word of it. It may even be good. Good? Genius! Stately pleasure dome! Caves of ice! This one will hit the anthologies for sure! …Uh oh… What if I forget it? What am I thinking? I'm a writer. I'll write it down. *(Sound of typing begins and continues, interrupted by the writer's exclamations.)* Sunless sea! Nicely turned…

decree, sea...This is fabulous—I don't even have to think! ...Mazy motion...ah! ...A miracle of rare device! I love it, and there's more. *(Sound of typing continues, softer, fading in and out...)*

MAN: *(He is almost finished eating. He takes out an address book, finds a number, picks up the phone.)* Operator?

(The OPERATOR'S VOICE *is amplified, but out of a hidden speaker [as with street sounds etc.] not* SPEAKER A *or* B.*)*

OPERATOR'S VOICE: Hello there, handsome. *(Sings)* What can I do, do do—For you, you youuuuuuu?

MAN: Could you try 555 404-7701 for me, please.

OPERATOR'S VOICE: Try? I'll simply ring the damn thing. Here you go, sweetheart.

(Phone rings. No answer. The MAN *hangs up.)*

MAN: Girl I used to know in this town. Long ago. Must be out. Or maybe she's moved away. *(He opens his fortune cookie. Reading)* "You are intelligent and sincere. You will go far in life." Yeah. Let me tell you, when you start losing your grip on things, if you get nervous and your hands get sweaty—then everything slides out and away. I can remember hanging on strong to all kinds of things...

You know, it is possible to devote your life to relieving other people's misery. People do it. It is also possible to devote your life to certain ideas. People do it. It is possible to devote your life to cultivating certain internal vibrations. People do it. Its also possible to just stand on the corner and take what comes. I thought I could never love enough, never shout loud enough, never be quiet enough, never go deep enough, or fast enough, or enough times to suit me. It's a wide highway, and you're following it and somehow it turns into a narrow alley, the houses crowding in on both sides. Surrounded. The earth quakes. Wells have gone dry. Piles of corpses are stacked up against the walls. We who are left split bones, and dig for the marrow.

(There is a knock on the door. Loud aggressive voice from the hallway, the LIGHTNING ROD SALESMAN*)*

LIGHTNING ROD SALESMAN: *(O S from outside door)* Sir or Madam! Better safe than sorry! BETTER SAFE THAN SORRY! Lightning rods for sale! All shapes, all sizes! Better safe than sorry? *(Knocking.)* Anybody home?

(The MAN *does not answer.)*

LIGHTNING ROD SALESMAN: *(O S)* Free brochure.

(The brochure flies in over the transom—a paper plane. The MAN *grabs it, glances at it, shows it to the audience, crumples it up and tosses it away. Steps of the* LIGHTNING ROD SALESMAN *fading away down the hall.)*

MAN: Insane.

SPEAKER B: *(Sound of a rhythmic knock on the door, soft.)*

SHELLEY (B): Who is it?

*(*GAIL *is* SHELLEY*'s age, nineteen or so, and* COUNTRYBOY *is a few years older. The sound of their voices should be more mature that* SHELLEY*'s.)*

GAIL (B): It's us, Shelley. Open up. *(Sound of door opening, people entering.)*

SHELLEY (B): Am I glad to see you guys. I been calling and calling.....

GAIL (B): They cut the phone off. We don't need the damn thing anyway. Jimmy around?

SHELLEY (B) I been sick, Gail

COUNTRYBOY (B): Where's Jimmy?

SHELLEY (B): I don't know. He hasn't been here for a week. Gail, I'm trying to tell you...

COUNTRYBOY (B): Shelley, you got a Dr Pepper or something… You got some M & Ms for the Country Boy? Anything sweet.

SHELLEY (B): I haven't been out. There's just water, down the hall in the bathroom. You want some?

COUNTRYBOY (B): Yeah, I want some.

SHELLEY (B): O K. I'll be right back. *(Sounds of door opening, her footsteps fading as she walks down the hall.)*

GAIL (B): Will you stop being so damn ugly?

COUNTRYBOY (B): You don't get it. She's gonna be sick for a long time. She's got nothing.

GAIL (B): I told you, Her mother sends her something every month…

(Sound of SHELLEY *returning, door opening.)*

SHELLEY (B): I got you the…

*(*SHELLEY *coughs harshly. Sound of her falling, glass breaking.)*

GAIL (B): Jesus. Country, get her up on the bed, hah…

*(*SHELLEY*'s crying, sobbing.)*

SHELLEY (B): You guys can find me something.

COUNTRYBOY (B): The drugstore is closed, darling, I am carrying nothing.

SHELLEY (B): Pretty please, Country. Jimmy took everything when he split. I even had a taste I was saving in this little perfume bottle. He took that too.

(The MAN *continues to listen intently.)*

GAIL (B): Baby, you're like ice. You got another blanket in here?

SHELLEY (B): You can get me something. Country, you got some cottons in our shirt pocket. I know you do….

COUNTRYBOY (B): If I could find you something, what am I gonna pay with, darling. I'm broke. Even if you had the bread, nobody's holding. Downtown, anyway. I ain't about to get myself killed on Lenox cause you got the shakes.

SHELLEY (B): ...there's a twenty in that top drawer... under the sweater... Country, take it, please.

COUNTRYBOY (B) All right. I'll do what I can. Maybe I can find some yellows, something to take the edge off.

SHELLEY (B): I love yellows. I'd like to go to sleep.

COUNTRYBOY (B): Gail, you coming?

GAIL (B) Shelley, you eat anything today?

SHELLEY (B): Yeah, I ate soup.

COUNTRYBOY (B): Gail, I'm out the door here.

GAIL (B): Lemme get my shoes on, dammit.

COUNTRYBOY (B): Don't worry, darling. The countryboy always comes back with something.

(Sound of door slamming as GAIL *and* COUNTRYBOY *leave* SHELLEY*'s room.)*

MAN: Oh Lord. If they come back to her, I'm Elmer Fudd.

*(*MAN*'s phone rings. As it rings, the dim shadow of an old man appears on the window shade behind him. He picks up.)*

OPERATOR'S VOICE: It's for you, sweetface. Hold a moment, while I patch you in. This one's long distance, to say the least.

MAN: I'm holding.

FATHER ON PHONE: *(Voice of* MAN*'s* FATHER.*)* Hello, son?

MAN: Dad? Is that you?

FATHER ON PHONE: Who else would bother?

MAN: But you're dead.

FATHER ON PHONE: What are you, prejudiced? Listen, there's a message for you. Came while you were out, from one of your girlfriends, I think. Let me find it here. Your mother must have put it on the… Ah. I got it. "Call Linda."

MAN: That's it? That's the message?

FATHER ON PHONE: Yeah. "Call Linda."

MAN: Who's Linda?

FATHER ON PHONE: How should I know?

MAN: Dad, when did you get that message?

FATHER ON PHONE: Don't ask about whens. I'm dead, remember. And another thing. I don't want you wasting your life. It's not only stupid—I don't like it, understand. Do what's right, and don't get crazy. Understand?

(The shadow on the shade begins to fade away…)

MAN: Yeah, but Dad, listen. I seem to have messed up a little here. Maybe you can…Dad? Dad? *(He jiggles the button, but its clear the phone's gone dead. He calls the operator.)* Operator?

OPERATOR'S VOICE: Sock it to me, dreamboat.

MAN: That call I just got, the connection…I got cut off. Do you have the number or anything?

OPERATOR'S VOICE: That call was from Deadland, sweetheart, and the connections never last long. I'll see if I can buzz the party. Uno momentito, slugger. *(Buzzings and clickings from the phone)* No luck, big shoulders. Trying to reach anyone over there is a hassle. They've got one switchboard for the entire joint, and sometimes no one's on duty. You're just ringing the air, blue eyes.

MAN: My eyes are green.

OPERATOR'S VOICE: You keep making these fine distinctions, buster, its gonna cost you. *(Click as the phone line goes dead. The man hangs up.)*

SPEAKER A: *(Sound of feverish typing, interrupted by exclamations of delight.)*

WRITER (A): Ah! Perfect! Damsel with a dulcimer! *(Sounds from* SPEAKER A *continue very softly.)*

MAN: *(Gesturing toward* SPEAKER A*)* He's found something to do. Keeps him happy sometimes. I used to be a salesman. Like that madman who was in the hallway. I guess I still am, if my company still exists. Door to door worker, selling Feldman's Original Books of Knowledge, a set in twenty-two volumes. Help you to the world's wisdom. Help your kid through school. Gonna deny your child this invaluable opportunity for learning? *(Taking a volume out of suitcase)*
The damn thing is actually a blurry photo-offset job on cheap paper, of the 1892 edition of the Encyclopedia Britannica, with every other article missing. Actually, not bad. I sold the damn thing in every little town along the route of the Canadian Pacific—Montreal to Vancouver. Train, hotel, do the town, back on the train. Train, hotel, do the town, back on the train. If they bought, I gave 'em one book, took a down payment, then filed their order with Feldman in the main office. The company was supposed to do the rest, mail a book a month and collect their money. The people I sold were poor, and thought the books would help their kids. In the end, they could never afford the whole set, so they'd stop paying, and the books would stop coming. I don't think Feldman even had any volumes beyond S... Border towns in Canada are deficient in the knowledge of things like Tasmania, and Utopias, and Velvet, and Weathervanes, and Xenophobia, and

Yuletide, and Zinc… *(Holding up the volume.)* A. *(He begins to read…)*

SPEAKER A: *(Sound of typing rises. Sharp knock on the door, followed by the voice of the lightning rod salesman from the hallway.)*

LIGHTNING ROD SALESMAN (A): Sir or madam? Sir or madam? A moment of your time! Better safe than sorry! *(Repeated knocking. Typing stops. Sound of door opening.)*

WRITER (A): What is it, dammit?

LIGHTNING ROD SALESMAN (A): Thank you, sir. My demonstration will only take a moment. *(Sound of closing door.)*

WRITER (A): I don't recall inviting you in.

LIGHTNING ROD SALESMAN (A): You need not make excuses, sir. In my business rudeness is commonplace. I represent the Porlock Lightning Rod Company. Save yourself from nature's white flash of death.

WRITER (A): Please. I'm in the middle of the most wonderful piece of work of my life. I'm really not inter…

LIGHTNING ROD SALESMAN (A): SIR! Lightning is far more common than you suppose. At this very moment, a thundercloud boils with a negative charge, building in potential till that probing lance of massed electrons sets out in quest of the victim below. Sir, there is even a type of lightning that concerns itself with direct attacks on the human brain. Comes right at your head. To make it shit simple for you, sir—next storm, you end up fried meat. Now a simple personal lightning rod that can be worn directly on the body can insure that you and your loved ones are guarded against the ravages of wild electricity. The rods are made of genuine copper plated plastic, and come with a Velcro clip to attach them securely to your person. Every rod is prepared under rabbinical supervision, and has been blessed by the pope. Let me demonstrate how comfortable....

WRITER (A): GET OUT!

LIGHTNING ROD SALESMAN (A): Pardon me?

WRITER (A): Get out of my hotel room, NOW! Before I smash your face, sir!

LIGHTNING ROD SALESMAN (A): Disgusting. A fellow human being offers to help you save yourself from natural disaster, to preserve your life and sanity, and you treat him like an animal.

WRITER (A): GET OUT!!!

(Slamming of a door. Footsteps of the LIGHTNING ROD SALESMAN *fade down the hallway. Sound of typing beginning again, hesitating, then stopping. The* MAN *is listening intently now.)*

WRITER (A): My god. Its gone. That idiot drove the poem out of my head... Nothing. I remember nothing. My head's as empty as a balloon. Shit. And the dam things not finished... It just stops in the middle. Hell, maybe it can just end there... *(Reads)* Beware! Beware!
His flashing eyes, his floating hair!
Weave a circle round him thrice,
And close your eyes with holy dread,
For he on honey-dew hath fed,
And drunk the milk of Paradise.

(Light fades on SPEAKER A.*)*

MAN: Not bad. *(He puts volume A of the Book of Knowledge back in his sample case.)* I quit. I tried to call Feldman at the office to tell him to get another boy, but the phone's been disconnected.

My last sale. There was this very sunny morning, really supernaturally bright sunshine, and everything in the world looked lit. And I was going door to door, and the people who opened them that one morning looked radiant and fine somehow—a man with a towel over his shoulder, half-shaved, blinking in the sunlight, little girl with a doll under her arm, a woman with her hair in curlers, smell of coffee floating out of kitchens, lawns getting mowed, and this sparkle on everything, like I was in a crystal world. And it was a sure thing to me that morning that these people had in them all the light in the world, and intelligence and humor and peace glowed in their eyes. All this was in a town called Bent Fork, in Alberta. So, it looked to me like selling a Book of Knowledge to these godlike creatures with their families and chores and work and play and children and earth and sky, would be just like selling the old refrigerator to the Eskimos, like teaching monkeys to climb trees, like looking for water by brushing away the waves…

SPEAKER B: *(*SHELLEY *coughs, then moans as if in pain. She is sobbing, then manages to stop herself. She sings, in a little child's voice…)*

SHELLEY (B): *(Singing)*
Uncle John is very sick, what shall we send him?
Three good wishes, three good kisses, and a slice of
  ginger.
Who shall we send it by, by the ferryman's daughter.
Take her by her lily-white hand and lead her over the
  water… *(She is sobbing, and then the sound fades…)*

MAN: Oh God…

So, I was saying, I stood there in the middle of town like a man from Mars, holding my sample case full of books under one arm, and I figured I'd try one more house. I knock. This woman comes to the door, and I don't think she's more than twenty-five, and she's got a dustpan in one hand, and her hair's tied up on her head some way, and she's got freckles running across her nose, and she's beautiful. She says come in, and I can see her ass moving under this thin dress she's wearing, and she wants to hear all about Feldman's Book of Knowledge, and before you know it we're in bed upstairs, banging away. She's real excited and having a great time, and I'm doing O K myself, but sort of wondering what's happening since this wasn't particularly my idea. So all the rubbing and oohing and ahhing is over, and she gets up, and its early afternoon, and she pulls her dress back on, and she says don't you think you better get out of here. We're in the bedroom and her husband's stuff is lying all around. In fact, I trip over one of his shoes climbing out of bed, a dark brown loafer. I ask her if she wants to buy Feldman's Book of Knowledge and she says are you kidding and get out of here dammit the kids'll be home from school any minute. I put my clothes on all right, but I don't leave. I'm happy there. She's angry, and after all that loving she sure enough hates me now, but I don't leave, and the kids come home, and their names are Ellie and Daniel, and they look like good kids to me and she tells them I'm a man selling books and they look at them and the house feels comfortable all around me and I can hear some birds chirping in the backyard and I sit in a chair in the living room. She's fixing dinner, putting a roast beef in the oven and I go in and watch her, and she looks over at me and says you're crazy you know, but I don't feel crazy one bit. Soon her husband comes home from work, and he's got this little moustache and he works in a sporting goods store, and they hug each other, and he shakes my hand, and invites me to dinner and the food's great, and I'm telling 'em about my travels, and after dinner I'm playing a game called Submarine Chase with Daniel and I can hear them arguing in the kitchen about me and who I am, and I can see I'm bringing fear and lying and no love here, and so I say excuse me, Daniel, and I pick up my sample case and go out on the porch. Its night, and a dog barks somewhere, and the Canadian Pacific through train to Vancouver whistles, pulling out of Bent Fork. I walk down to the station, I lie down on a bench. There'll be another train in the morning...

That was my last day on the job. If anyone here wants a set of Feldman's book of Knowledge, I'm sorry but I no longer sell them. Find Feldman, if you can.

You know, it's a fact, and it goes to show you. You work at it, and work at it, and you get a little older and you figure out what you've bought with all that effort. You bought death. Somehow you got it backwards. It's life you been trying to buy, Death you're supposed to get for free.

SPEAKER C: *(Sharp knocking on* SHELLEY*'s door.)*

SHELLEY (B): Country? Country? Gail? Is that you? *(Knocking again)* Who is it?

LIGHTNING ROD SALESMAN (B): It's the lightning rod man! Is your Mommy home?

SHELLEY (B): No.

LIGHTNING ROD SALESMAN (B): Open the door and let me in!

SHELLEY (B): No!

LIGHTNING ROD SALESMAN (B): Safe and sound. Last chance at this price. Shelley, let me in, or I'll pick up my sample case, walk down the stairs and out, into the street, where I'll be hidden from you forever.

*(*SHELLEY *does not answer.)*

LIGHTNING ROD SALESMAN (B): Goodbye.

Sound of the lightning rod man's footsteps going down the stairs, fading…)

SHELLEY (B): *(Singing, slowly)*

Oh Mary Mack, mack, mack, all dressed in black black black

With silver buttons, buttons, buttons all down her back back back

She asked her mother, mother…

(She stops singing. We hear her talking now, in a very small voice…) …Oh, Mom, I'm so sick…can I stay home from school today…please…I'm sorry, I'm so sorry…

MAN: *(To himself)* Shelley, please stop crying. The man on the other side of the wall is checking out, and I'm hoping someday I'll look back over my shoulder and you'll be running to catch up to me, and I'll wait there in the road for you—

*(*SPEAKER B*''s light fades. The* MAN*'s phone rings. He picks up.)*

OPERATOR'S VOICE: Hello handsome. One moment for Madame!

LANDLADY: *(On phone)* Listen you cheap chiseler! Pack your shit and get out of my room! Now! You hear me?

MAN: I hear you, I'm going.

LANDLADY: *(Phone)* And another thing! If you're jerking off in the room, that's three bucks extra! You hear me!

MAN: I have ears.

LANDLADY: *(Phone)* You're going now?

MAN: Yeah.

LANDLADY: *(Phone)* The world's a wonderful place. I remember it. Stay sober. There's no need to check out. I'm crossing you off the book right now. There. You're gone.

(Click of the LANDLADY *hanging up the phone. The* MAN *hangs up.)*

MAN: It goes to show you. You can spend the time you're given playing around in the shallows, or you can dive deep and swim with the fishes. I am gonna disappear now, a spot of snow floating down into the fire. If you blink just once in your coffin you'll miss me. You won't even see me go.

Cowshit becomes tomatoes, piss becomes rain, petals of roses turn to black soil, comets into sparklers that burn away in the air, young girls into old women, ink into dust, dead trees to diamonds, and stones into sand on the shore. My turn now.

(He stands, straightens his tie, picks up his suitcase, then drops it onto the floor. He picks up the plant on the windowsill, touches its dirt—dry. He looks around for water—none. He spits into the plant pot, watering it with his saliva. He places it back on the sill. He picks up the Gideon Bible, goes to put it in its drawer, stops. He sticks his finger into the book at random, opens it to that page. Reading:)

"For ye shall go out with joy, and be led forth with peace: the mountains and the hills shall break forth before you into singing, and all the trees of the field shall clap their hands." Yeah.

*(*MAN *puts the Bible in its drawer, leaves the room. Strong light rises through the windowshade. The shadow of a pigeon appears, is there a moment, and is gone.)*

SPEAKER A: *(Sound of typing begins, hesitant at first, then consistent and strong. This sound fades slowly as all lights, including the circular fluorescent on set, fade to black.)*

(Lights up on the M C, *with other performers nearby.)*

M C: Our show, Limbo Tales, such as it is, has ended. My associates and I commend ourselves to you, and we humbly beg your pardon if our tongues stumbled into anyone's happiness. It's rare enough in this world. These sorry clowns and I have played the lives of nameless men in a dance before you. You've seen, in your mind's eye, the great Count Orloff, Art Hubble, and the Bold Grimace Boy. I ask you to love them all, with their faults, as if they were your own children. In any heap of coins you can find a piece of silver, even gold.

When you go home tonight, safe in bed, see them all once again, in your dreams.

We are only travelers. We pass beneath thy hands, beneath thy feet.

Thank you. Goodnight ladies, goodnight gentlemen, goodnight.

(All bow.)

END OF PLAY

www.ingramcontent.com/pod-product-compliance
Lightning Source LLC
LaVergne TN
LVHW010548100826
845148LV00013B/2653

9780881455540